T0117473

DID YOU KNOW?

"Secrets Mothers Never Tell Their Grown Children"

Annie Durham

authorHOUSE®

AuthorHouse™
1663 Liberty Drive
Bloomington, IN 47403
www.authorhouse.com
Phone: 1-800-839-8640

© 2012 Annie Durham. All rights reserved.

No part of this book may be reproduced, stored in a retrieval system, or transmitted by any means without the written permission of the author.

Published by AuthorHouse 8/2/2012

ISBN: 978-1-4772-5373-1 (e)
ISBN: 978-1-4772-5374-8 (sc)

Library of Congress Control Number: 2012913479

Any people depicted in stock imagery provided by Thinkstock are models, and such images are being used for illustrative purposes only.
Certain stock imagery © Thinkstock.

This book is printed on acid-free paper.

Because of the dynamic nature of the Internet, any web addresses or links contained in this book may have changed since publication and may no longer be valid. The views expressed in this work are solely those of the author and do not necessarily reflect the views of the publisher, and the publisher hereby disclaims any responsibility for them.

<u>INTRODUCTION</u>

This is a book for mothers of grown children and those children. Maybe, it's about time we understood each other a little better. Moms, don't be mad at me for spilling some trade secrets. Maybe some of these apply and some don't, but one thing we share, for certain, is our grown children really have no idea, do they?

FOREWARD:

Mothers everywhere have secrets;
some we have when our kids are
small. Some we have when they are
teens. Still others, we keep from
our children who are "adults". I may
be breaking all the rules, here, but
I am going to let you in on them.

WARNING: You are about to enter into
the world of Mothers, it is not for the
faint of heart, nor the easily frightened.

This book is dedicated to

my three children:

Melissa, Kyle and Katie

You are the best thing I have

ever done or ever will do. I have

made many mistakes. But you still

need to listen to your mother!

*I love you for all time and beyond.

DID YOU KNOW?

That just because you're my grown child — you're still my <u>child.</u> It is not a reflection of your maturity or abilities. It is an irreversible, biological fact. You are lodged permanently in my heart's largest artery...That is why, when you scare me, I can't breathe!

DID YOU KNOW?

Just because I don't strap you into your car-seat anymore, doesn't mean I don't look sideways, out of my left eye, to see if you attached your seatbelt, as you pull out of my driveway, since you've told me you don't want me reminding you anymore.

<u>DID YOU KNOW?</u>

My mind has been known to wander

to your Digestive or Excretory

system during the day, hoping

all is coming out, as it should.

Scared yet?

(Oh, we're just getting started.)

DID YOU KNOW?

When you go to the beach or
outside, I want to call and remind
you to keep reapplying your
sunscreen, so you don't have to
deal with skin cancer, later in life.
But you would just get mad,
so I don't, but I want to.

DID YOU KNOW?

I hope my voice plays, screechingly, in your head, when you get behind the wheel, if you or your friend has been drinking. I want my face and voice to cause you so much pain, as to render you blind and incapable of being in anything other than a cab.

DID YOU KNOW?

When you call and tell me you're going to the store, mall or the gas station; I'm already praying that there is no one in the parking lot that would want to do you harm. Sorry, that's just the way I roll ☹

DID YOU KNOW?

I wonder if you take the time to marvel at and thank the Creator for his creations? And if you remember, how to go to him, at any hour, for he loves you so?

Yep, I pray for that too☺

<u>**DID YOU KNOW?**</u>

I pray that God guards your tongue,
so you don't bring unwanted
trouble into your life, as I've
done so many times in mine.
Words are so much easier
going out, than when we try
to put them back again☹

<u>DID YOU KNOW?</u>

That I also pray, that when the time
comes, and it will, when you have
to stand for what is right, even
though it is unpopular, remember- a
backbone is a beautiful thing and
far too uncommon, these days.

Of course, you know the Lord has your
back and so do I. I don't care if I'm 90;
mess with my baby and it's on! Oh,
the purse will be just a-swinging!

DID YOU KNOW?

That I still wonder, sometimes,

if you remember your company

manners, when you're a guest in

someone's home? I know you're

rolling your eyes, as you read this.

As my Daddy always said, "Raising Tells".

<u>DID YOU KNOW?</u>

When I don't even enter your mind, I am talking to God about you and I often ask him to let you "run into" Godly people who will bless your life. I also pray that you will be one of those people, in other's lives.

DID YOU KNOW?

I've asked God to give me cancer

or accidents, or fear, if it means he

could keep it from you. I've told him

I understand that going through

disappointment and loss, is the way

we learn and grow and change for the

better, but to <u>please</u> hold your hand,

every minute, while you are going

through it- because I can't. (He must

think I'm crazy, praying for what he

already gives you, but there you have it.)

<u>DID YOU KNOW?</u>

Sometimes your Dad gets mad at me
for worrying about you, now. But I
think he's finally come to accept –
<u>it's not gonna change.</u> You better
ride that acceptance train too!

I'm sorry, did I say worrying?
I meant caring greatly☺

DID YOU KNOW?

I can appear perfectly normal, to those around me, and be in the middle of asking God to put his angels all around you and perform my duties without a hitch! You'd never know.

That's just what we Moms do.

<u>DID YOU KNOW?</u>

If it were legal and/or realistic, I would vote you in, as President, because I trust your heart.

*Well, maybe we could start with you being my V.P. (baby steps)

<u>DID YOU KNOW?</u>

Even though I am lying in my bed, late at night and you are, only God knows where...In my mind and heart, I am tucking you in. I am soothing your brow, pushing those wayward strands of hair, back where they belong, kissing your forehead and pulling the covers up to your chest, and singing, singing, singing to you.

Really.

And... I am praying that because I can't tuck you in, that God will; that because I am not in the room, that he will occupy that chair in the corner, and if a tear should slip down your cheek for whatever reason, he will wipe it away.

That should you wake, in the night, like you did, as a child....That you know, the light is on and you need only to call my name or walk down the hall, into my arms – even if we're miles apart. You see, the light is always on, in my heart and even when God calls me home, the part of me that is your Mom, will always be alive and beating and loving you.

DID YOU KNOW?

That even though I may be ridiculous, annoying or you fill in the adjective_____, I am your number one fan. I've paid for season tickets on the 50 yard line of your life. I'm not there to take your place nor play for you, but to stay there…. long after the coaches, refs and other fans leave – to tell you, you are the best, no one can replace you and that come, rain, shine or cancellations, scores, fouls, wins or losses…

I will still be there. <u>I will not give up my seat.</u> I will be right where you left me. I don't care where you are, I'm in the stands, watching your game.

You can see me, just look up. I'm the heart beating with your every breath and the heart is wearing a T-shirt, with your picture on it.

(Yep, the one you hate.)

Oh and one more...

DID YOU KNOW?

That just because you think I've

let you in on the secret thoughts

mothers have for their grown

children, DID YOU KNOW...

We've got more.

*We'll always be one step

ahead of you, darlings.

Love,

Mom

<u>Notes from Your Mom:</u>

DID YOU KNOW?

_____

_____

_____

_____

_____

_____

_____

_____

_____

_____

_____

DID YOU KNOW?

_____

_____

_____

_____

_____

_____

_____

_____

_____

_____

_____

_____

DID YOU KNOW?

_____

_____

_____

_____

_____

_____

_____

_____

_____

_____

_____

DID YOU KNOW?

_____

_____

_____

_____

_____

_____

_____

_____

_____

_____

_____

DID YOU KNOW?

_____

_____

_____

_____

_____

_____

_____

_____

_____

_____

_____

DID YOU KNOW?

_____

_____

_____

_____

_____

_____

_____

_____

_____

_____

_____

_____

DID YOU KNOW?

_____

_____

_____

_____

_____

_____

_____

_____

_____

_____

_____

_____

DID YOU KNOW?

_____

_____

_____

_____

_____

_____

_____

_____

_____

_____

_____

_____

DID YOU KNOW?

_____

_____

_____

_____

_____

_____

_____

_____

_____

_____

_____

_____

DID YOU KNOW?

_____

_____

_____

_____

_____

_____

_____

_____

_____

_____

_____

_____

Printed in the United States
By Bookmasters